This Is a Let's-Read-and-Find-Out Science Book®

FOSSILS TELL OF LONG AGO

REVISED EDITION

BY ALIKI

THOMAS Y. CROWELL　　NEW YORK

For Jason
who found the fossil that inspired the book

With thanks to Katherine Tegen,
and to William S. Simpson of the Field Museum,
for their help

———————————

The *Let's-Read-and-Find-Out Science Book* series was originated by Dr. Franklyn M. Branley, Astronomer Emeritus and former Chairman of the American Museum–Hayden Planetarium, and was formerly co-edited by him and Dr. Roma Gans, Professor Emeritus of Childhood Education, Teachers College, Columbia University.

Let's-Read-and-Find-Out Science Book is a registered trademark of Harper & Row, Publishers, Inc.

FOSSILS TELL OF LONG AGO

Copyright © 1972, 1990 by Aliki Brandenberg
Printed in the U.S.A. All rights reserved.
1 2 3 4 5 6 7 8 9 10
Revised Edition

Library of Congress Cataloging-in-Publication Data
Aliki.
  Fossils tell of long ago / by Aliki. — Rev. ed.
    p.   cm. — (Let's-read-and-find-out science book)
  Summary: Explains how fossils are formed and what they tell us about the past.
  ISBN 0-690-04844-0 : $. — ISBN 0-690-04829-7 (lib. bdg.) : $
  [1. Paleontology—Juvenile literature.   2. Fossils.] I. Title. II. Series.
QE714.5.A43 1990   89-17247
560—dc20   CIP
                                                                       AC

FOSSILS TELL OF LONG AGO

Once upon a time a huge fish was swimming around
   when along came a smaller fish.
The big fish was so hungry it swallowed the other fish whole.
The big fish died and sank to the bottom of the sea.

This happened ninety million years ago.

How do we know?

We know because the fish turned to stone.

The fish became a fossil.

A plant or animal that has turned to stone is called a fossil.

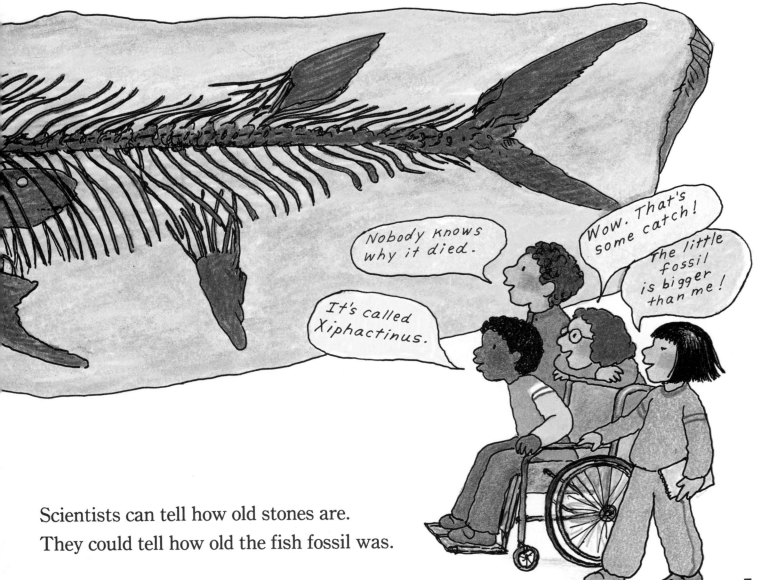

Scientists can tell how old stones are.
They could tell how old the fish fossil was.

7

How did the fish become a fossil?
Most animals and plants do not become fossils when they die.
Some rot.

Pe-YOOO-eee!

Others dry up, crumble, and blow away.
No trace of them is left.
This could have happened to the big fish.
We would never know it had lived.
Instead, the fish became a fossil.
This is how it happened.

When the big fish died, it sank into the mud at the bottom of the sea.

Slowly, the soft parts of the fish rotted away.

Only its hard bones were left.

The bones of the fish it had eaten were left, too.

The skeleton of the fish lay buried and protected deep in the mud.

Thousands of years went by.

More layers of mud covered the fish.

Tons and tons of mud piled up.

After a long time, the surface of the earth changed.

The sea where the fish was buried dried out.

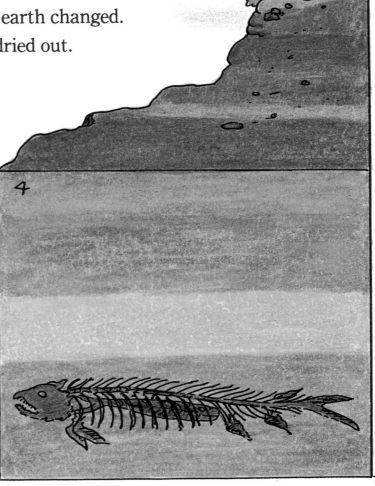

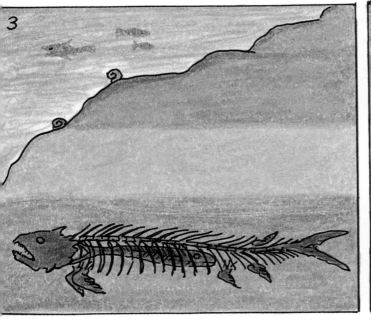

The weight of the layers of mud pressed down.
Slowly, the mud turned to rock.
As that happened, ground water seeped through the changing
 layers of mud.
Minerals were dissolved in the water.
The water seeped into all the tiny holes in the fish bones.
The minerals in the water were left behind in the fish bones.
After a very long time the bones turned to stone.
The fish was a fossil.

Some fossils, like the fish, are actual parts of plants or animals
   that have turned to stone.
Sometimes a fossil is only an imprint of a plant or animal.

Millions of years ago, a leaf fell off a fernlike plant.
It dropped onto the swampy forest soil, which is called peat.
The leaf rotted away.
But it left the mark of its shape in the peat.
The peat, with the imprint of the leaf, hardened.
It became a rock called coal.
Coal is a fossil, too.

Peat is made up of mushy, rotted leaves.

We use peat in the garden to make plants grow.

NEUROPTERIS
(seed fern)

PEAT

15

It's
Iguanodon!

These are dinosaur tracks.

They were made in fresh mud 115 million years ago.

Sand filled the dinosaur's footprints in the mud.

The sand hardened into a rock called sandstone.
Millions of years later fossil hunters dug through the rock.
They found the fossil tracks—exact imprints of the dinosaur's foot.

Not all fossils are found in stone.

Some are found in the frozen ground of the Arctic.

This ancient mammoth was a kind of elephant.

It froze to death thousands of years ago.

The grass it had been eating was still in its mouth!

Millions of years ago a fly was caught in the sticky sap of a tree.
The sap hardened and became a fossil called amber.
Amber looks like yellow glass.
The fly was perfectly preserved in the amber.

Other insects have been preserved in amber, too.

We have learned many things from the fish,
the fern, the fly, and the dinosaur tracks.
Fossils tell us about the past.

Fossils tell us there once were forests where now there are deserts.

Fossils tell us there once were seas where now there are mountains.

Many lands that are cold today were once warm.
We find fossils of tropical plants in very cold places.

Fossils tell us about strange creatures
that lived on earth long ago.
No such creatures are alive today.
They have all died out.
We say they are extinct.

Some fossils are found by scientists who dig for them.

Some fossils are found by accident.
You, too, might find a fossil if you look hard.
When you see a stone, look at it carefully.
It may be a fossil of something that once lived.

I found this fossil at the seashore.

Lucky!

It says you can find fossils in the woods, too.

Or where they just dug a new road.

Or up in the mountains.

We saw fossils in the marble walls of a big building.

Marble is polished limestone where many fossils have been found.

I want to find a fossil.

How would you like to make a fossil?
Not a one-million-year-old fossil.
A one-minute-old fossil.
Make a clay imprint of your hand.

The imprint shows what your hand is like, the way
a dinosaur's track shows us what its foot was like.

Suppose, when it dried out, you buried your clay imprint.

Suppose, a million years from now, someone found it.

Your imprint would be as hard as stone.

It would be a fossil of your hand.

It would tell the finder something about you.

It would tell something about life on earth a million years earlier.

31

Every time someone finds a fossil, we learn more about life
on earth long ago.
Someday you may find a fossil—one that is millions and millions
of years old.
You may discover something no one knows today.